A Rainbow Book

Black
English
Vernacular

(From "Ain't" to "Yo mama")

The Words Politically Correct Americans Should Know

Monica Frazier Anderson

Rainbow Books, Inc.

Library of Congress Cataloging-in-Publication Data

Anderson, Monica Frazier, 1962-
    Black English Vernacular : from "ain't" to "yo mama" : the
words politically correct Americans should know / Monica
Frazier Anderson.
        p.   cm.
    Includes index.
    ISBN 1-56825-005-3 : $8.95
    1. Afro-Americans-Language (New words, slang, etc.)-
-Dictionaries. 2. English language—United States—Slang-
-Dictionaries. 3. Black English—Dictionaries. 4. Americanisms-
-Dictionaries. I. Title.
PE3727.N4A53 1994
427' .0089'96073—dc20   93-48032
                                                              CIP

Black English Vernacular
(From "Ain't" to "Yo mama")
The Words Politically Correct Americans Should Know

Copyright © 1994 by Monica Frazier Anderson
Interior & Cover Design: Betsy Lampé
Cover photo: Otis Smith / make-up: Everette Lyles
Published by Rainbow Books, Inc.
                    P. O. Box 430
                    Highland City, FL 33846-0430
                    Telephone: (813) 648-4420

Manufactured in the United States of America.

With love and gratitude, this book is dedicated to Alfred, Tony, Adrian, Gladys Arcolia and Jimica.

Introduction

Black English Vernacular (BEV) is the everyday language commonly spoken by African Americans in social settings. It is the informal language of African Americans and members of other ethnic groups who have been strongly influenced by African-American culture.

It is difficult to define BEV succinctly because, like Standard English, it is a living language that adapts and evolves with the changing society. Yet, the core of this language ... syntax, pronunciation, verb usage, inflection and non-verbal enhancers ... are well-established conventions. It is not at all difficult to identify someone who is speaking or imitating BEV.

It is much easier to state what BEV is *not*. It is *not* bastardized Standard English (SE). While it may have *initially* been derived from SE centuries ago, by slaves attempting to master a foreign tongue, it has *since* become its own entity. In fact, for some users it is a conscious rejection of SE. BEV is no more "bad English" than Italian is "bad Latin."

BEV has only recently begun to attract scholarly scrutiny. Indeed, it is predominantly a *spoken* language, which makes it all the more difficult to research. Many African-American authors, such as Langston Hughes and Terry McMillan, have successfully documented BEV through the characters in their work. But for millions of Americans and non-Americans, BEV remains a mystery.

At the heart of this mystery lies the fact that professional African Americans generally avoid speaking BEV in the work place or in social settings where they are in the minority. In order to ensure that their thoughts are clearly conveyed and interpreted, they adopt the language common to all Americans, SE. In the same manner, a person from Europe uses the term "soccer" instead of the European "football" when addressing a group of Americans on the subject. Were he addressing a group of his countrymen, even on American soil, he would not hesitate to use the term "football," and they would not misunderstand.

This type of "juggling" is merely a matter of expediting communication by adopting the "general" language for a general audience.

It is a standing joke among African Americans:

"Did you know that I'm bilingual?"

"Really?!"

"Yes. I speak black *and* white." Ha, ha, ha.

This book is not intended to *teach* BEV. In fact, African Americans, by and large, are insulted by non-African Americans who attempt to imitate BEV. The offender is guilty of "trying to act black."

This book is merely a translation, a dictionary of sorts, of the most commonly, currently used words and idioms or phrases in BEV. These words and phrases are more than time-dated slang. Slang is transitory. Most of these contents have existed for generations and now fall into the category of "standard usage."

The main point to keep in mind is that, while the words are not new or different, the meaning behind them is, indeed, quite unique in most cases. Read this book with an open mind and a sense of humor. BEV is a *fun* language. Upon completion, I hope you'll agree that the problem many non-African Americans have in understanding BEV is that they become mired in the unconventional usage of one or two words and fail to listen to the entire sentence or paragraph. Most of the time, the context of the statement will give you a good idea of the meaning of the "foreign" word.

Please join me in celebrating Black English Vernacular as another savory ingredient in our delicious American stew.

-Word-

Dr. M. F. Anderson

The
Words
and
Phrases
of
Black
English
Vernacular

Words and Phrases

"AIN'T"

Pronunciation: (aynt)
*S.E. Syn.: no, negative

Example: "I *ain't* seen Pearl in years," or "I *ain't* playing with you no more."

(The word *ain't* may denote present or past tense. The word does not change form; the tense is derived from modifiers.)

"AIN'T NO TELLING"

S.E. Syn.: to be unpredictable

Example: "*Ain't no telling* when this trial will end."

* Standard English Synonym

"AIN'T THAT A BITCH?"

S.E. Syn.: I'm stunned. This is unbelievable."

Example: "Julia Roberts married Lyle Lovett. *Ain't that a bitch?*"

"AMEN CORNER"

S.E. Syn.: a group of church elders who continuously say, "*amen,*" during a sermon in order to convey their endorsement of the pastor's message

Example: "*Sister* Jenkins *been* sitting in that *Amen Corner* for thirty years."

"ASHY"

Pronunciation: (**ash** e) *adjective*
S.E. Syn.: dry skin that has a chalky appearance on dark-skinned people

Example: "You need some lotion for them (your) *ashy* legs."

Words and Phrases

"BACK"
"BOOTY"

Pronunciation: (**boo** te) *noun*
S.E. Syn.: buttocks, rear end

Example: "*Check it out!* Do girlfriend got much *back* or what?" "Tyrona's *booty* is so big she might be able to loan you some of the extra."

(In the African-American community, it is generally preferable to have a nicely round but firm rear end. Flat rear ends are below standard.)

"BAD"

Pronunciation: (bad) *adjective*

S.E. Syn.: good, excellent, outstanding

Example: "Tyrone's new jacuzzi is *bad!*"

"BANK"

Pronunciation: (bank) *noun*
S.E. Syn.: wealth, affluence

Example: "Honey, this new job means big *bank* from now on."

"BEADY HEADED"

S.E. Syn.: a male with dry, short, unmanageable hair that is in an infinite number of tight, little curls that resemble B.B.s in a B.B. gun

Example: "You tell that *beady-headed* Calvin to rake the yard right now!"

"BE"
"BEEN"

The verb "to be" is usually not extensively conjugated in BEV. Pluralization and tense are shown by the subject and number.

Examples: "She *be* lying to him all the time." "People don't *be* at the club 'til eleven o'clock." "I *been* sitting around here all day."

"BIGMAMA"

S.E. Syn.: grandmother

Example: "*Bigmama* Lucile will turn eighty tomorrow."

"BOGARDING"

Pronunciation: (**bo** gar din) *verb*
S.E. Syn.: interfering, interrupting

(From Humphrey Bogart, known for his tough guy antics.)

Example: "Raymond keeps *bogarding* the game. I'm gonna tell Mama Rose if he don't quit!"

"BONES"

Pronunciation: (bonz) *noun*

S.E. Syn.: dominoes

Example: "We played *bones* for four hours yesterday."

"BOOGIE"
"BOOGIE DOWN"

Pronunciation: (**boo** gee) *verb*
S.E. Syn.: to have a good time, party; To leave

Examples: "We *boogied* until the wee hours of the morning. That was a great batchelor party." "I'm afraid I'm going to have to *boogie* ... I have an appointment." "We gonna *boogie down* tonight, mama."

"BOOMING SYSTEM"

S.E. Syn.: an extraordinary stereo system with speakers capable of emitting levels of sound harmful to human ears.

Example: "Leroy has a *bad booming system* in his car."

"BOURGEOISIE"

Pronunciation: (boorz **wha**) *noun, adjective*

S.E. Syn.: materialistic; member of the middle or upper classes; also known as *"High falluting"*

Examples: "Eloise is so *bourgeoisie* that she eats cornbread with a fork." "Them *high falluting* sorority girls get on my nerves."

"BROKE YOUR FACE"

S.E. Syn.: to embarrass or humiliate someone

Example: "She *broke your face* so bad you need to be quiet for the rest of your life."

"BROTHER(S)"

Pronunciation: (**bru** thers) *noun*

S.E. Syn.: generic, universal reference to black males; title of respect which precedes the Christian name when addressing male church members; fraternity member

Examples: "That sure is one fine looking *brother*." "*Brother* Jaleel is taking the collection." "The *brothers* of Phi Beta Sigma are fine and intelligent too."

"BUMP THAT!"

S.E. Syn.:   to deliberately ignore

Example: "They want us at practice at 6 a.m. on a Saturday? *Bump that*, I'll be way off in dream land."

"BUST A CAP"

S.E. Syn.:   to kill someone with a gun

Example: "Arista *bust a cap* on her fiance last night."

"BUST A MOVE"

S.E. Syn.:   to take action; to intervene

Examples: "If you coming with us, homeboy, you need to *bust a move*." "She's too pretty to dance with him. I'm gone *bust a move*."

(It is customary to delete the final consonants in words. i.e. "you" for "you're," or "talkin'" for "talking.")

"BUSTED"

Pronunciation: (**bust** id) *verb*
S.E. Syn.: to be caught in the act of being unfaithful
            to a spouse or loved one; arrested

Examples: "She *busted* him when she came home
           early from her business trip." "He got
           busted for driving while intoxicated."

"BUSTING SUDS"

S.E. Syn.: washing dishes
Example: "I can't play right now, mama got me
          busting suds. I'll be outside later."

Words and Phrases

"CALL ME OUT OF MY NAME"

S.E. Syn.: to insult with profanity

Example: "The next time you *call me out of my name*, the good Lord won't be able to save you."

"CAUGHT IN THAT BAG"

S.E. Syn.: to be obsessed with something or someone

Example: "He's *caught in that* materialistic *bag*; clothes, jewelry and cars."

"CHECK IT OUT"
"CHECK THIS OUT"

S.E. Syn.: listen; look at this (see "Peep this")

Examples: "I got my class ring today. *Check it out.*"
"*Check this out,* this is the rought draft of my speech."

"CHILD"

Pronunciation: (chil) *noun*

S.E. Syn.: preface to addressing a female of any age; a youth

Examples: "*Child,* did you watch *Oprah* yesterday?"
"Come here, *child,* and put on some shoes."

"CHILLING"

Pronunciation: (**chil** lin) *verb*
S.E. Syn.: to relax

Example: "Tonight, I'm just *chilling* at the *crib.*"

"CHITTERLINGS"

Pronunciation: (**chit** lins) *noun*

S.E. Syn.: a culinary dish consisting of pig intestines
See "Soul Food"

"CHUNK"

S.E. Syn.: to throw

Example: "I can *chunk* a rock farther than you."

"CLEAN"

S.E. Syn.: nice, pretty (see "Sharp")

Example: "My new ride is too *clean*." "Your leather suit *show* is *clean*."

"COOL"

Pronunciation: (kool) *adjective*
S.E. Syn.: genteel; extraordinary; congenial

Examples: "Emily Post is so *cool*." "That's the *coolest* watch I've ever seen." Don't get upset. We *cool*."

"COPPING Zs"

S.E. Syn.: to sleep or nap

Example: "I worked eighteen hours today. All I want

to do now is *cop* some *Zs*."

"CREW"

Pronunciation: (kru) *noun*

S.E. Syn.: close friends; constant companions (see "Posse")

Examples: "My *crew:* me, Demond, and Trey, won a 3-on-3 tournament." "Every rap star has a *crew* of homeboys."

"CRIB"

Pronunciation: (krib) *noun*

S.E. Syn.: residence; domicile

Example: "Stop by the *crib* and pick me up on your way to school tomorrow."

"CUT OUT"

S.E. Syn.: to be unfaithful

Example: "Charles *cut out* on Tiffany last night."

Words and Phrases

"DAISY DUKES"

S.E. Syn.:   very brief shorts

Example: "That Arlene wears them *daisy dukes* clear up her *booty*."

(From the customary attire of Daisy Duke of the '70's television series, *The Dukes of Hazzard*)

"DAP"

S.E. Syn.:   to lightly tap your fist above or below another person's fist symbolizing approval or acceptance

Example: "Give me some *dap* homeboy. I see great minds think alike."

"DEF"
"DOPE"
"STUPID"

S.E. Syn.:   outstanding; fabulous

Example: "Those new Nikes you bought are *def.*" "This new video cam is *dope.*" "The stealth bomber is *stupid!*"

"DIGITS"

Pronunciation: (**di** jits) noun

S.E. Syn.:   telephone number

Example: "Baby, why don't you drop those seven *digits* on me?"

"DISSIN"

Pronunciation: (**dis** sen) *verb*

S.E. Syn.:   to make a scathing comment about a person or thing; to belittle

Examples: "Man, he was *dissin* your sister real bad."

"DO"

S.E. Syn.: hair style

Example: "I really like your new *do*, Shaniqua."

"DOG"

Pronunciation: (dawg) *noun*

S.E. Syn.: male friend (see "G"); unsavory male

Examples: "What's up *dog*?" "I hate him. He's nothing but a *dog*."

"DONE"

Pronunciation: (dun) *verb*

S.E. Syn.: has; have

Example: "We *done* talked enough! What part of 'no' don't you understand?"

"DON'T GO THERE"

S.E. Syn.: "Let's change the subject."

Example: "You probably know some of his deepest,
            darkest secrets but *don't go there* o.k."

"DON'T MAKE ME HAVE TO GO OFF ON YOU"

S.E. Syn.: "Don't make me angry. I'm not a nice
            person when I'm angry."

Example: "You're a pest. *Don't make me have to go off
            on you,* girlfriend."

"DON'T MAKE ME READ YOU"

S.E. Syn.: "You must not know who I am."

Example: "I've been banking here for ten years. *Don't
            make me read you,* girlfriend."

"DON'T SWEAT ME!"

S.E. Syn.: a warning; "Go to hell!" or "Stop it right
            now!" (see "I don't play that!")

Example: "I'm tired James. Just *don't sweat me.*"

"DOWN HOME"

S.E. Syn.: birth place, city; hometown

Example: "We went *down home* for a family reunion last weekend."

"DUDE"

S.E. Syn.: guy, man

Example: "I like that *dude's* tie."

"DUFUS"

Pronunciation: (**du** fus) *adjective*

S.E. Syn.: extremely stupid; clumsy; unattractive

Example: "Homeboy is so *dufus*. He's even got a *dufus*-looking car."

 # Words and Phrases

"FINE"

S.E. Syn.: physically attractive; comely

Example: "That man is too *fine* to be a stranger!"

"5.0"

Pronunciation: (five oh) noun

S.E. Syn.: police officer; police informant

Example: "Chill man, 5.0 is driving by." "Don't talk to him, he's 5.0"

(From the Mustang 5.0 litre driven by many patrol officers.)

"FLICTED"

S.E. Syn.: afflicted; clumsy, awkward

Example: "Why did you invite that *flicted* girl to sit at our table?"

"FLY"

S.E. Syn.: exceptional, outstanding (see "Fresh")

Example: "Monica is one *fly* woman. Not only is she beautiful, she's a dentist, too."

"FOR REAL THOUGH"

Pronunciation: (for reel doe)

S.E. Syn.: to be in accord; "I couldn't agree with you more." (see "I know that's right!")

Example: "*For real though*, baby, you know I love you. I was just *messin' with* that other girl."

"411"

Pronunciation: (four one one)

S.E. Syn.: news, information (see "Low down")

Example: "What's the *411* on that homicide last night?"

"FREAK"

S.E. Syn.: sexually uninhibited

Example: "Madonna is a pure *freak*."

"FRESH"

Pronunciation: (fresh) *adjective*

S.E. Syn.: new; innovative (see "Fly")

Example: "Quincy Jones' latest CD is *fresh*."

"FUNKY"

Pronunciation: (fun kee) *adjective*

S.E. Syn.: churlish; acrid; awesome

Examples: "That Louise better come off that *funky* attitude of hers." "Man, go take a bath ...

you got some *funky* feet." "Anita got some *funky* clothes from her boyfriend yesterday. She looks great."

Words and Phrases

"G"

S.E. Syn.: male friend; macho term of endearment (see "Dog")

Example: "Later, *G*." "Hey, *G*, how about picking up my mama for me."

"GACHT"

Pronunciation: (gat) *noun*

S.E. Syn.: semiautomatic weapon; gun; also known as chrome, AK (from AK-47)

Example: "I was terrified when he put that *gacht* to my head."

"GANGSTER"

Pronunciation: (**gang** stah) *noun*

S.E. Syn.: a criminal; a member of a gang

Example: "Stay away from Big Daddy. He's just another no good *gangster*."

"GEAR"

S.E. Syn.: stylish clothing

Example: "Arsenio Hall wears fresh *gear*. "How do you like my new top *gear* (shirt)?"

"GET DOWN"

S.E. Syn.: to be unreserved, especially while dancing

Example: "That's my favorite song. Let's *get down*!"

"GET IT ON"

S.E. Syn.: to begin, start; to make love

Examples: "The guest speaker is here, let's *get it on*."
"We can *get it on* all night."

"GIMME FIVE"

S.E. Syn.: An invitation to slap the outstretched palm of the speaker. The subsequent nonverbal communication may represent a greeting, praise for a noteworthy accomplishment, or agreement. Also known as *high five,* which is to perform this gesture above the head and *five low,* which is to perform this gesture at knee level.

"GIRLFRIEND"

S.E. Syn.: informal address; "My dear..." (see "Homegirl")

Example: "*Girlfriend,* it's time for you to wake up and smell the coffee."

"GIT WITH THE PROGRAM"

S.E. Syn.: to conform; "You are way out of line."

Example: "If you want to keep this job, you had better *git with the program!*"

"GIT WITH YOU"

S.E. Syn.: to establish a relationship; to make love; to consult (see "Step to you"")

Examples: "Miss lady, I show wanna *git with you* this evening." "Did he *git with you* last night, LaRhonda?" "I'll *git with you* on the details later."

"GIVING ME GRIEF"

S.E. Syn.: to harass; annoying, worrisome

Example: "My bossman be *giving me grief* every day."

"GOING WITH"

S.E. Syn.: dating

Example: "I been *going with* Theron since high school."

"GONE"

S.E. Syn.: is/are going to

Example: "We *gone* leave the house around noon."

"GOOD HAIR"

S.E. Syn.: a male or female with finely textured hair that is straighter in its natural state than average African-American hair.

Example: "All them Creoles got *good hair.*"

"GOT BURNED"

S.E. Syn.: jilted; damaged, hurt

Example: "Sonny's been depressed every since he *got burned* by Benita."

"GOT IT GOING ON"

S.E. Syn.: to have a privileged lifestyle; financially independent

Example: "Dr. Conrad and his wife really *got it going on.*"

"GOT OFF"

S.E. Syn.: a laudable performance

Example: "Michael Jordon *got off* in the game yester-
            day. He scored sixty points."

"GOT SMOKED"
"DUSTED"
"CLIPPED"

S.E. Syn.: to be murdered

Example: "The dude at the convenience store *got
            smoked* (dusted or clipped) by some guy
            with a knife."

"GREEK"

S.E. Syn.: a member of one of the eight historical,
            African-American sororities or fraternities:
            Zeta Phi Beta, Alpha Kappa Alpha, Delta
            Sigma Gamma, Sigma Gamma Rho, Phi
            Beta Sigma, Alpha Phi Alpha, Omega Psi
            Phi, Kappa Alpha Psi

Example: "I know you went to college. Are you *greek*?"

"GRUB"

S.E. Syn.: to eat

Example: "I'm gone *grub* until I bust on my birthday!"

Words and Phrases

"HAIR GREASE"
"GREASE"
"HAIR DRESSING"

S.E. Syn.: special oils used by some African-Americans to prevent excessive dryness of the hair and scalp; animal fat or vegetable oil used for frying foods.

Example: "After swimming, I always wash my hair and *grease* it to the scalp." "I can't believe that girl used hand lotion for hair grease!"

"HANG(ING)"
"HANG(ING) OUT"
"HANG(ING) WITH"

S.E. Syn.: to accompany

Example: "I can't go out with you tonight because I'm *hanging* with my homegirls."

"HARD"

Pronunciation: (hard) *adjective*

S.E. Syn.:   unfortunate; callous, unfeeling (also known as *stone cold*)

Example: "They lost everything in the fire. That's *hard.*"

"HE CAN'T BUST A GRAPE"

S.E. Syn.:   phrase used to imply that a male has diminuitive genitalia; egotism

Example: "He's all talk and no action; *he can't bust a grape.*"

"HE GOT THE BIGHEAD"
"SHE ACT LIKE HER SHIT DON'T STINK"

S.E. Syn.:   the person is very arrogant

Example: "Since Mike got rich, *he's got the bighead.*"

"HEIFER"

Pronunciation: (**hef** er) *noun*
S.E. Syn.: an insult to a female

Example: "That *heifer* seduced my old man."

"HIGH YELLOW NEGRO"

S.E. Syn.: a light-skinned African-American

Example: "What possessed that *high yellow negro* to wear a red suit."

"HINCTY"

Pronunciation: (**hank** te) *adjective*
S.E. Syn.: ostentacious; aloof; proud

Example: "She's so *hincty*, she drives with her legs crossed."

"HIS/YO RAP IS WEAK"

S.E. Syn.: one who does not have a persuasive style of speaking, particularly with ladies

Example: "I'm glad he can sing cause *his rap is so weak.*"

"HOLLER AT YA"

S.E. Syn.:   "I'll call you later."

Example: "I'll *holler at ya* after my anatomy class."

"HOMEBOY"
"HOMEGIRL"

S.E. Syn.:   a male or female friend; an acquaintance from the same community, city, state or country

Example: "I want you to meet my *homeboy*, Terrence. We went to elementary school together."

"HONKY"
"CRACKER"
"PECKERWOOD"
"OFAY"

Pronunciation: (**hongk** e) *noun*
S.E. Syn.:   derogatory label for a European-American

Example: "That *honky* security guard followed me all over the store, out to the parking lot, into my car, and when I got home, he called to make sure I had arrived safely."

"HOOD"

S.E. Syn.: neighborhood

Example: "The folks in the *hood* are planning a block party."

"HOOK ME UP"

S.E. Syn.: to make a connection

Example: "*Hook me up* with that *fly* girl over by the Coke machine."

"HOOPTY"

Pronunciation: (hoop **tee**) *noun*

S.E. Syn.: automobile, especially an older model (see "My ride")

Example: "I've got a thousand dollars worth of speak-
          ers in my *hoopty*."

"HOW COME...?"

S.E. Syn.: why?

Example: *"How come* you always late for work, *G?"*

Words and Phrases

"I AIN'T GOING OUT LIKE THAT"

S.E. Syn.: "I'm not taking all the blame." "I refuse to be a victim."

Example: "The cops think I killed that old lady but *I ain't going out like that.*"

"I DON'T WANT NONE OF YOUR LIP"

S.E. Syn.: to be quiet, cease speaking, no reply required

Example: "*I don't want none of your lip* about attending that party tonight."

"I/HOMEY DON'T PLAY THAT"

S.E. Syn.: expression of defiance or annoyance; veiled threat of retaliation (see "Don't sweat me")

Examples: "*I don't play that* cause I ain't scared of nobody." "*Watch your back*, man, Z-boy *don't play that.*"

"I KNOW THAT'S RIGHT"

S.E. Syn.: to concur, agree (see "For real though," "right on")

Example: "She really deserves the promotion," Jean commented.
"*I know that's right.* It's long overdue," Marie replied.

"I'LL BEAT THE BLACK OFF OF YOU!" "BOY, I'LL KNOCK YOU INTO NEXT WEEK!"

S.E. Syn.: "I am so angry with you."

Example: "You never should have taken the car without asking. You ever do that again and *I'll knock you into next week.*"

(Hyperbole, such as used in these expressions, is not to be taken literally.)

"ILLING"

Pronunciation: (**il** lin) *verb, adj.*

S.E. Syn.: to bother; unusual behavior (see "Why you tripping?")

Examples: "What's *illing* you, my brother?" "Your sister be *illing* sometimes."

"I'M AUDI"

S.E. Syn.: to take leave of (see "Take it easy")

Example: "Everyone around here is too tense for me, *I'm Audi* you guys."

"I'M DOWN WITH THAT"

S.E. Syn.: to be in harmony (see "Word")

Example: "*We down with that* plan of action. Let's do it."

"I'M GONE BUST YOU UPSIDE THE HEAD"

S.E. Syn.: a warning, usually figuratively speaking

Example: "*I'm gone bust you upside the head* if you forget your lunch money again!"

"I'M ON"

S.E. Syn.: I'm going to

Example: "*I'm on* write a letter to my congressman about Proposition 19."

"I'M SERIOUS AS A HEART ATTACK"

S.E. Syn.: "I'm not lying. This is the absolute truth."

Example: "The car really is gone, daddy. *I'm serious as a heart attack.*"

"I'M THROUGH WITH YOU"

S.E. Syn.: "I'm at a loss for words."

Example: "You've been named the new District Attorney! Girl, *I'm through with you.*"

"IN THE HOUSE"

S.E. Syn.: to be present

Example: "We gone to start this thing out right, we got Adrian Craig *in the house* tonight."

"IT DON'T TAKE ALL THAT"

S.E. Syn.: phrase used to describe unwarranted behavior; "That's absurd"

Example: "That meeting lasted over four hours. *It don't take all that.*"

"IT'S"

S.E. Syn.: there are; it is

Example: "*It's* at least a hundred people in the audience tonight."

"IT'S (A)BOUT TIME!"

S.E. Syn.: "My goodness, what took you so long!"

Example: "It's *'bout time* you showed up with that newspaper!"

Words and Phrases

"JACKED"

S.E. Syn.: robbed, i.e. carjacked; humiliated, i.e. jacked up

Examples: "Bodine got *jacked* for his Rolex yesterday." "Man, Earl got *jacked* at the gym. His mama came in there looking for him after school, and boy was she ticked off."

"JAM"
"JAMMIN'"

S.E. Syn.: to celebrate, as in a party; extraordinary production, especially music (also known as "Slammin," "On the One")

Examples: "Let's go to the Kappa's Bahama pajama *jam.*" "Man, you should have been at the club last night. The band was *jammin'*."

"JIMMIE"

Pronunciation: (**jim** mee) *noun*

S.E. Syn.: penis

Example: "I had her begging for the *jimmie*."

(This euphemism was coined by rap artists so that they could describe sexual exploits while being censored by the FCC.)

"JUKE JOINT"

S.E. Syn.: a small bar and/or dance hall

Example: "My son loves that sorry *juke joint*."

"JUNGLE FEVER"

S.E. Syn.: an uncomplimentary diagnosis of an African-American who prefers to have intimate relationships with someone of another race, particularly a white person

Example: "Look at that Uncle Tom. He's *gone* die from that *jungle fever*."

Words and Phrases

"KICK(ING) IT"

S.E. Syn.: to begin; to relax (see "Let's get busy")

Example: "We should have started thirty minutes ago. Let's *kick it*."

"KITCHEN"

S.E. Syn.: area of the hairline above the nape of the neck

Example: "You need to take a (hair)brush and work on that nappy *kitchen*."

"KNOCKING BOOTS"

S.E. Syn.: sexual intercourse (also known as "Doing it," and "Bumping nasties")

Example: "Man, me and my old lady spent all night long *knocking boots*."

Words and Phrases

"LAWS"

S.E. Syn.: the police

Example: "Them *laws* always be giving me parking tickets."

"LIGHTEN UP"

S.E. Syn.: an admonishment to be more optimistic; "Look on the bright side"

Example: "We're going to make this work, Mike. Please, just *lighten up*."

"LOOK OUT!"

S.E. Syn.: a greeting (see "What's up?" "Word up!")

Example: "I'm home family! *Look out!*"

"LOW DOWN"

S.E. Syn.: news, information (see "411"); cowardly, devious

Examples: "What's the *low down* on the referendum?"
"He's a *low down*, no good thief."

Words and Phrases

"MACK DADDY"

S.E. Syn.: debonair; self-aggrandizing term used by males to convey superiority

Example: "I'm the *Mack Daddy*, and I run this *hood*."

"MAIN SQUEEZE"

S.E. Syn.: boyfriend; lover

Example: "This is Byron. He's my new *main squeeze*." "Me and my *main squeeze* are gone go and do the *nasty* tonight."

"MAKE GROCERIES"

S.E. Syn.: to shop for groceries

Example: "I'm out of meat and canned goods. I need to *make groceries*."

"MAMA THEM"

Pronunciation: (**ma** ma dem)

S.E. Syn.: "My mother and her companions..."

Example: "*Mama them* went to the mall."

"MCGYVER"

S.E. Syn.: to attempt or accomplish an impossible feat as in the television program of the same name

Example: "He ran the forty in four seconds flat! Man, that's *McGyver*."

"MEDDLING"

Pronunciation: (**med** lin) *verb*

S.E. Syn.: to tease; to interfere

Example: "Mama, Junior keeps *meddling* me. Tell

him to quit it." "You quit *meddling* in other people's business."

"MESSED OVER"

S.E. Syn.: to victimize, dupe; depreciate; to do half heartedly

Examples: "He show *messed over* that woman. She never should've trusted him." "That apartment got *messed over* bythe last renters." "The choir sure *messed over* that song."

"MESS WITH"

S.E. Syn.: to bother

Examples: "Don't *mess with* me, Trey. I'll hurt you."

"MIX"

Pronunciation: (miks) *verb*

S.E. Syn.: to begin, to start; to fight; to enhance

Examples: "The rally hit the *mix* when we came." "Well, if you're so bad, let's *mix* it up!"

"When we put more bass in the *mix*, the music is better."

"MOTHERLAND"

S.E. Syn.: Africa

Example: "Every African American should visit the *motherland.*"

"MY BAG"

S.E. Syn.: "Sorry, my mistake."

Example: "Aw, baby, I thought you liked chocolate-covered ants. Oh well, *my bag.*"

"MY OLD LADY"
"MY OLD MAN"

S.E. Syn.: my wife/husband; my mother/father (also known as "Old hen," for the feminine)

Example: "*My old lady* likes fresh flowers."

"MY RIDE"

S.E. Syn.: my automobile, car (see "Hoopty")

Example: *"My ride* is the baddest in the hood."

Words and Phrases

"NAPPY"

Pronunciation: (**nap** pee) adjective

S.E. Syn.: kinky, tightly curled hair that is difficult to comb

Example: "You could use a good perm on that *nappy* head."

"NIGGER"

S.E. Syn.: stupid, oaf; a generic label used by some African Americans to refer to other African Americans; however, because of the negative connotations, this practice is increasingly frowned upon

Example: "*Nigger*, get your feet off my table."

(The word "nigger" is considered an insult when used by a non African American.)

"NIGGER, PLEASE"

Pronunciation: (**nig** gah plez)

S.E. Syn.: "You're kidding!"

(*Extreme caution advised.* Under no circumstances should a non-African American use the word "nigger" when speaking to an African American!)

 # Words and Phrases

"ON MY/HIS JOCK"

S.E. Syn.: a coquettish female, a flirt

Example: "Man, that girl was *on your jock* so bad, if you'd gone to the bathroom, she would have fallen off your zipper."

"OREO"

Pronunciation: (**or** e o) *noun, adjective*

S.E. Syn.: negative description of one who eschews their African-American heritage, (a figurative reference to Oreo cookies, which are black on the outside, but white on the inside); African American who is continuously in the company of European Americans

Examples: "That *oreo* thinks his ancestors came here
          on a yacht."

Words and Phrases

"PEACE"
"PEACE OUT"

S. E. Syn.: farewell

Example: "Ya'll take care. I'm gone, *peace out.*"

"PEEP THIS"

S. E. Syn.: listen to me (see "Check this out")

Example: "Yo man, *peep this* scripture. It's deep."

"PLAYER"

Pronunciation: (**pla** uh) *noun*

S. E. Syn.: someone who dates a lot of different women; a pimp

Examples: "I use to be a *player*, but now I'm a one-woman man." "All the *players* want a Benz like Don Juan's."

"PLAYING THE DOZENS"

Pronunciation: (**pla** in da **duz** inz)

S. E. Syn.: phrase used to describe contemptible behavior of one party toward a second party (from *The Dirty Dozen*); descriptive phrase of a tradition whereby two or more parties repeatedly exchange personal insults, often for the entertainment of bystanders, also known as "Casing," "Hoorahing" and "Highsiding"

Examples: "She's so disloyal, always *playing the dozens*." "They had everyone laughing when they were *playing the dozens*."

"PODNER"

Pronunciation (**pod** nuh) *noun*

S. E. Syn.: best friend, sidekick; partner

Examples: "Alfred, meet my *podner* Beau." "I always vacation with my *podner*." "Will, be my *podner* for a quick game of bones."

"POSSE"

S. E. Syn.: one's social circle; close friends or companions (see "Crew")

Examples: "I'm spending spring break with my *posse*." "Can't we go on a date without your *posse* sometimes?"

"PRAYER WARRIORS"

S. E. Syn.: avid Christians who battle adversity by praying constantly

Example: "I'll find a job soon. I put my *prayer warriors* on notice."

"PROPERS"

Pronunciation: (**prop** ers) *noun*

S. E. Syn.: courteous regard, respect; "Kudos"

Example: "Carl worked diligently to earn his college degree. He deserves his *propers*."

"PUNK"

Pronunciation: (punk) *adjective, noun*

S. E. Syn.: timid, fearful; effeminate

Example: "That *punk*, Warren, can't even go to the bathroom without his wife's permission."

Words
and
Phrases

"QUE"
"Q"

S.E. Syn.: barbecue

Example: "Let's grill some ribs tonight. I'd love some good *que.*"

Words and Phrases

"RAGGEDY"

Pronunciation: (**rag** ge dee) adjective

S.E. Syn.: dilapidated; old

Example: "This school building is so *raggedy* roaches won't come here."

"RAGS"

S.E. Syn.: nice clothing (also known as "Threads," "Duds")

Example: "I got new *rags* for my date with Candy."

"RAP"

S.E. Syn.: to speak rhythmically with musical accompaniment; to converse; a pick-up line

Examples: "Tevin can sing but he can't *rap* at all."
"Watch me win this lady over with my smooth *rap*."

"RAW"

S.E. Syn.: intense

Example: "My love (for you) is so *raw*."

"RIGHT ON!"

S.E. Syn.: an affirmation (see "I know that's right!")

Example: "We got to stop killing each other. *Right on, brother*!"

"ROCK STAR"
"ROCK MONSTER"

S.E. Syn.: a crack cocaine addict

Example: "She used to be an attorney, but now she's just another *rock star*."

"RUNNING BUDDY"

S.E. Syn.: ally, associate; friend

Example: "Me and Ezekiel been *running buddies* since the first grade."

(The word "have," as in "have been," is often omitted.)

Words and Phrases

"SANG"

S.E. Syn.: present tense of "sing," (also known as "Blow")

Example: "That girl can *sang*! She sounds like an angel."

(Vowels are sometimes modified to show excitement or to add emphasis.)

"SAY WHAT?"

S.E. Syn.: "Are you kidding?"

Example: "*Say what?* You got fired again!"

"SCHOOL YOU"

S.E. Syn.: to teach or elaborate (also known as "Break it Down")

Example: "If you want to make friends in this office, just let me *school you.*"

"SCRAPPING"
"SQUABBLING"

S.E. Syn.: fist fight

Example: "Dough Boy and Ice T gone *scrap* after school today."

"SEDITY"

Pronunciation: (su **di** te) *adjective*

S.E. Syn.: an arrogant female (see "Hincty")

Example: "That *sedity* heifer gets on my nerves."

"SHARP"

S.E. Syn.: extraordinary; striking (also known as

"Tough," "Sharp as a tack") (see "Clean")

Example: "That suit she's wearing is *sharp*."

"SHE AIN'T ABOUT NOTHING"

S.E. Syn.:   to be without amibition, no future

Example: "S*he ain't about nothing.* She been *gone* start a business for six years."

"SHE MADE A BABY FOR HIM"

S.E. Syn.:   she's pregnant

Example: "*She made a baby for him* and he *ain't* never admitted to being the daddy."

"SHE PUT HER FOOT IN THEM..."

S.E. Syn.:   phrase used to describe someone who is an excellent cook

Example: "Mabel sure *put her foot in them* greens. They're the best I've ever had."

"SHE THINKS SHE'S SOMETHING"

S.E. Syn.: arrogant; aloof (see "He got the bighead")

Example: "*She thinks she's something* cause she drives a BMW."

"SHOOTING BLANKS"

S.E. Syn.: description of a male who is unable to impregnate his wife

Example: "Denise has been trying to make a baby for five years. Thomas must be *shooting blanks*."

"SHOUTING"

S.E. Syn.: to be so overcome by religious fervor that you have a strong physical reaction, which includes crying, yelling and jumping (also known as "Got happy," "Got the Holy Spirit")

Example: "She was *shouting* so hard her wig fell off."

"SHOW"

Pronunciation: (sho) *adverb*

S.E. Syn.: surely; really; indeed

Examples: "He *show* is crazy." "*Show* you('re) right
          girlfriend."

"SHOW NUFF"

S.E. Syn.: to concur; really

Example: "Girl, you're *show nuff* right."

"SNATCH"

S.E. Syn.: to grab suddenly

Example: "I s*natched* the toddler out of the seat just
          in time."

"SOLID"

S.E. Syn.: yes, a good idea

Example: "Meet me here after dinner." "*Solid.*"

"SOUL FOOD"

A "fifth" food group, consisting of vegetables, meats and desserts which tend to be highly seasoned. These menu items were the staple foods of the slaves and they have remained popular among people of African descent. Favorite food items include collard greens, turnip greens, chitterlings, sweet potato pie and hot water cornbread.

"SPADES"

S.E. Syn.: a popular card game in which the suit of spades is always trump.

Example: "Get the cards and let's play some *spades*."

"SPLIT"

S.E. Syn.: to leave; to end a relationship or split up

Example: "Jeannie and John have *split*. I wonder who'll get the car?"

"STANDING IN THE GAP"

S.E. Syn.: intercessory prayer by devoted Christians

on behalf of a sinner

Example: "Helen has no family to help her so we're *standing in the gap.*"

"STAY BLACK"

S.E. Syn.: farewell; a reminder to be proud of one's African-American heritage and culture (see "Word to the mother")

Example: "*Stay black* and don't forget where you came from."

"STEP OFF"

S.E. Syn.: Leave me alone, you're annoying me.

Example: "*Step off* before I call security."

"STOP FRONTING ME"
"PUTTING ON A FRONT"
"PERPETRATING"

S.E. Syn.: to end the pretense

Example: "Our marriage is over, Ben, *stop fronting me.*"

"STRAIGHTENING HAIR"
"STRAIGHTENING COMB"

S.E. Syn.: a hot metal comb

Example: "That *straightening comb* is too hot, you'll burn your hair."

(The straightening comb was invented by Mrs. C. J. Walker, who became the first African-American female millionaire.)

"STRAIGHT UP"

S.E. Syn.: "Would I lie to you?"

Example: "*Straight up*, sir, this is the lowest price on this item in the entire city."

"STYLING"

Pronunciation: (**sti** len) *adjective*

S.E. Syn.: fashionable, attractive

Example: "Girl, you are really *styling* in those daisy dukes." "Your new do is *styling*, Katrina."

"SUCKER"

Pronunciation: (**suk** ah) *noun*

S.E. Syn.: despicable character; a gullible person

Example: "That *sucker* doesn't care about anyone but himself."

"SUGAR IN HIS COFFEE"

S.E. Syn.: effeminate; gay

Example: "If you ask me, he's got a little too much *sugar in his coffee*."

"SUNDAY-GO-TO-MEETING CLOTHES"

S.E. Syn.: semi-formal attire

Example: "You must have an interview. Where are you going in your *Sunday-go-to-meeting clothes*?"

Words and Phrases

"TAKE IT EASY"
"SEE YOU LATER" (*LA TAH*)
"I'M OUTTA HERE"

S.E. Syn.: farewell

Examples: "It's past my curfew guys, *take it easy*."
"*See you later*, my ride is here."

"TALKING SMACK"

S.E. Syn.: to address someone in a disrespectful manner or tone

Example: "My dad would stomp me for *talking smack* like that."

"TALK TO ME!"

S.E. Syn.:   respond; give feedback; answer

Example: Phone rings ... "*Talk to me,* this is Shiela."

"TESTIFY"

S.E. Syn.:   to recount a blessing you have received

Example: "Sisters and brothers, God's been good to me. I want to *testify* this morning."

"THAT'S COLD (BLOODED)"

S.E. Syn.:   to be ruthless; callous disregard for others

Example: "He abandoned his pregnant wife on their first wedding anniversary. *That's cold.*"

"THAT'S FAT"
"THAT'S BAD"

S.E. Syn.:   a compliment

Example: "*That's a fat* new *ride* you've purchased."

"THE DEVIL IS WHIPPING HIS WIFE"

S.E. Syn.: a meteorological phenomenon occurring when the sun is shining brightly but it's also raining at the same time

Example: "Folks need sunglasses and an umbrella when *the devil is whipping his wife.*"

"TIGHT"

S.E. Syn.: inseparable; very loyal friends

Example: "Bruce and Moe been *tight* since pre school."

"TOM"
"SELL OUT"

S.E. Syn.: obsequious; spineless, weak

Example: "That (uncle) *Tom* is going to break his damn back trying to kiss somebody's ass one day."

"TOOK HIM OUT"

S.E. Syn.: to defeat in battle

Example: "He kept on *messing with* me so I *took him out*."

"TORE UP"

Pronunciation: (tow up)

S.E. Syn.:   to be drunk or high on drugs; to be upset

Example: "Gary was so *tore up* he couldn't drive."

"TRIFLING"

Pronunciation: (**trif** lin) *adjective*

S.E. Syn.:   silly, frivolous

Example: "Leslie dropped out of high school to hitch-hike across Europe. She is so *trifling*."

"TURNED IT OUT"

S.E. Syn.:   a boast; to be the best

Example: "Me and my *posse* won first place in the talent show. We *turned it out*."

Words and Phrases

"WATCH YOUR BACK"

S.E. Syn.: be careful

Examples: "*Watch your back,* man, these cross town rivalries are serious."

"WENT LEFT"

S.E. Syn.: to have lost one's composure

Examples: "Chief Kennard *went left* on Sargeant Carter."

"WHACK"

Pronunciation: (whak) *adjective*

S.E. Syn.: ridiculous, ludicrous; pathetic

Examples: "His proposal was *whack*. They want forty percent of our earnings."

"WHAT'S UP?"

Pronunciation: (whuz up)

S.E. Syn.: a greeting; "Hello, how are you? I'm glad to see you." (see "Look out!," "Word up!")

Example: "*What's up*, James? I *ain't* seen you since the war."

"WHAT'S UP WITH THAT?"

S.E. Syn.: "Please explain your irrational behavior. Exactly what is going on here?"

"WHERE YOU AT?"

S.E. Syn.: "Where are you?" (location)

Example: "I can't pick you up until I know *where you at*."

(It is legitimate to end a sentence with a preposition.)

"WHERE YOU STAY?"

S.E. Syn.:   "Where do you live?"

Example: "I see you in the park all the time. *Where you stay?*"

"WHO IS YO FOLKS/PEOPLE?"

S.E. Syn.:   "What does your father do?" (occupation)

Example: "You from around here boy? *Who is yo folks?*"

"WHY YOU TRIPPING?"

S.E. Syn.:   "You're acting really strange. What's wrong with you?"

Example: "We've done this a thousand times. *Why you* keep on *tripping?*"

"WITNESS"

Pronunciation: (**wit** nes) *verb*

S.E. Syn.: Christian practice of telling atheists, agnostics, and non-Christians about God.

Example: "Everyone that joins that church has to *witness* twice a week."

"WORD"

S.E. Syn.: to concur; to agree; "Uh huh" (see "I'm down with that")

Example: "If I was able, I'd give Susan Lucci an Emmy myself." "*Word,* she deserves one."

"WORD TO THE MOTHER"

S.E. Syn.: a farewell with the specific intent of conveying respect for the motherland (Africa) (see "Stay black")

Example: "Don't say 'goodbye,' say '*Word to the Mother,*' brother."

"WORD UP!"

S.E. Syn.: a greeting (see "What's up?" "Look out!")

Example: "*Word up!* Jerome is *in the house.*"

"WORE HER/HIM DOWN"

S.E. Syn.: to be weakened emotionally and physically

Example: "Working two jobs for so long finally just *wore her down.*"

Words and Phrases

"YO"

Pronunciation: (yo) *noun*

S.E. Syn.: a greeting; a plea for attention

Examples: "*Yo* man, what's up?" "*Yo.* Can I get some help in here?"

"YOU AIN'T NEVER GONE (A)MOUNT TO NOTHIN', BOY!"

S.E. Syn.: "Son, you have no ambition, whatsoever. You're hopeless."

Example: "Hundred dollar tennis shoes and no job. *You ain't never gone (a)mount to nothin', Boy!*"

(Use of double negative is very common in BEV.)

"YOU AIN'T NEVER LIED"

S.E. Syn.: to concur; to endorse or second an expressed opinion; "That's the truth, the whole truth, and nothing but the truth." (see "For real though," "I know that's right")

Example: "She do look like an ostrich. *You ain't never lied.*"

"YOU BETTER CHECK YOURSELF"

S.E. Syn.: "Think before you act in haste and commit a grave error."

Example: "Drinking and driving is dangerous. *You better check yourself.*"

"YOUNG BUCK"

S.E. Syn.: a male youth

Example: "The average *young buck* in a gang won't live to see his thirtieth birthday."

"YOUR MAMA"

Pronunciation: (yo **ma** ma)

S.E. Syn.: strong insult; a retort; a veiled invitation to fight

Example: "You got those clothes from the flea market." "*Your mama.*"

"YOU SO TIRED"

S.E. Syn.: an expression of disgust, loathing; "You're pathetic."

Example: "I can't believe we're related. *You so tired.*"

"YOU THE MAN"
"I'M THE MAN"

S.E. Syn.: praise for superior achievement

Example: "Straight A's and perfect attendance, *you the man.*"

"Now the whole world had one language and a common speech . . .

"The Lord said, 'If as one people speaking the same language they have begun to do this (build the Tower of Babel), then nothing they plan to do will be impossible for them. Come, let us go down and confuse their language so they will not understand each other.'

"So the Lord scattered them from there all over the earth, and they stopped building the city. That is why it was called Babel ... because there the Lord confused the language of the whole world."

Genesis 11:1-9

About the Author

Monica Frazier Anderson is wife, mother, dentist, football *aficionado* and writer. She has been a columnist for the Minnesota *Viking Update* and the Cincinnati *Bengal Update*, and a staff writer for the *Leaguer*. She has also written for *Raising Minnesota*, *Northwest Dentistry* and the *Minneapolis Star Tribune*, as well as being a featured guest on *Twin Cities Live*, *Good Company*, *The Herschel Walker Show*, *Between Friends*, and *Crimestoppers*.

Dr. Anderson has a Bachelor of Science degree in Biology from Baylor University, Waco, Texas. She graduated from the University of Minnesota School of Dentistry in 1988.

Dr. Anderson is currently living in Arlington, Texas, where she continues to contemplate Black English Vernacular in the very politically correct sense of the word!

Black English Vernacular
by Monica Frazier Anderson

For additional copies of *Black English Vernacular*, telephone TOLL FREE 1-800-356-9315. MasterCard/VISA/American Express accepted.

To order *Black English Vernacular* direct from the publisher, send your check or money order for $8.95 plus $3.00 shipping and handling ($11.95 postpaid) to Rainbow Books, Inc., P. O. Box 430, Highland City, FL 33846-0430.

For *quantity purchases*, telephone/fax Rainbow Books, Inc., (813) 648-4420 or write to Rainbow Books, Inc., P. O. Box 430, Highland City, FL 33846-0430.